AJINKYA
RAHANE COLOR

MR VIVEK KUMAR PANDEY
SHAMBHUNATH

ISBN 979-888530091-9

Short biography of Ajinkya Rahane and about life ,during writing this book no character & no religious are harmed written by mr vivek kumar pandey. winner youngest writer award 1st rank in india 2020.He is only one writer can publish 700+ own book that was greatest successfull in his life.this book fully colour edition books.

Contents

Foreword

Author biography in English :MY NAME IS VIVEK KUMAR PANDEY . I WAS BORN IN 30 SEP 2002,I AM FROM SURAT GUJARAT INDIA.MY DREAM WAS TO BE GOOD WRITERS ,MY FAMILY SUPPORTED ME TO SUCCESSFUL AND I CAN DO IT MY SELF.How do I write? That is a question, I believe, that cannot be honestly answered by me."CELEBRATING YOUNGEST WRITER AWARD WINNER IN GUJARAT 1ST RANK" MR PANDEY JI . I may think I did a good job writing something when in reality it could be horrible. The reader is the one who decides the quality of my writing. I do not find writing to be natural to me and therefore find it to be a real challenge. My trick as a challenged writer is to do the best I can and know that I am happy with the final outcome. It may take a while to do my best and there may be quite a few problems I run into along the way.

I am not a greedy person those who are thinking about me and my self I never tried it anyone people suffering from sadness ,I trying to get promoted people suffering from happiness and joy in your Life Time. Now in current situation in India and also world people are unemployed and have no many but our indian governor help to people to get free food from ration card , i also take part in leadership team ,i am Motivational speaker , Film script writer. There was my two dream firstly writer and secondly actor & also my own film is upcoming soon i done almost completely completed script for my film .I AM GOING TO SAY WORD OF HEART TOUCH OUT PLEASE READ IT" , firstly i thanks my father he supports me in this field they always getting inspired me by own his words and behavior ,they always said that he was a biggest person in the world in future and also they purchase fruit and chocolate for me in anytime & anyway , firstly my father buy him then call me Vivek you want a chocolate i will say yes papa but how many tell me ,papa: you tell me how much i buy him i told 1 or 2 chocolate but my father purchase whole the boxes of chocolate and they get suprised me. MY FATHER WAS BORN IN " 20 SEPTEMBER" 1971 IN INDIA.

1) MY FATHER FAVORITE CLOTHES IS KURTA PAIJMA AND ALSO STYLES SHOE

2) FAVORITE SINGER IS KISHORE DA

3) FAVORITE STATE GUJARAT AND KOLKATA , HIS VILLAGE IN BIHAR

4) FAVORITE COLOR BLACK AND WHITE

THEY ALSO LOVE cricket like IPL and one day t-20 .they also like watching a News daily and heard the song daily ,they also interested in tik tok video but in current time tik tok is banned in india but also few videos are in you tube. In lockdown time my family and me very enjoy day daily. my father play daily ludo with his sister and son, daughter.they always loved tea and coffee anytime call me "। वविके थोडा़ चाय बनाओना वविके तमु्हारे हाथ का चाय अच्छा लगता है". I make it tea for my father but some reason after the April to june they are suffering from fever and cough , weakness on 6 June 2020 my father death. they not told me say bye bye his life. After death of 6 June on 10 june my mom and dad anniversary.but my father is Best in the world they can do anything for me please take care of father and respect it of your parents

CHAPTER ONE

Ajinkya Rahane Colour

- Ajinkya Rahane

Ajinkya Madhukar Rahane (born 6 June 1988) is an Indian international cricketer. He is vice-captain of the Indian cricket team in Test cricket. He played primarily as a middle-order batsman in the Test format and as a top-order batsman in white-ball forms of the game.He represents Mumbai in domestic cricket and Delhi Capitals in IPL.

Rahane made his first-class debut in 2007–08 Ranji Trophy season for Mumbai. He made his international debut in a T20I against England at Manchester in August 2011. Rahane made his Test debut in the March 2013 Border–Gavaskar Trophy. His first Test century came at Basin Reserve, Wellington against New Zealand. Under his captaincy, India won the 2020-21 Border–Gavaskar Trophy in Australia. As of May 2021 Rahane ranks 15th in the ICC Test batting rankings, with a tally of 688 points.

- Early and personal life

Rahane was born on 6 June 1988 in Ashwi KD, Sangamner Taluka, Ahmednagar district to Madhukar

Baburao Rahane and Sujata Rahane in a Hindu Maratha Family.[He has a younger brother and sister, Shashank and Apurva Rahane. At the age of seven, Madhukar Rahane took Rahane to a small coaching camp with a matting wicket in Dombivli,[as they could not afford proper coaching.From the age of 17, he took coaching from former India batsman Pravin Amre. Rahane cleared his Secondary School Certificate from SV Joshi High School, Dombivli.

Rahane married Radhika Dhopavkar, his childhood friend, on 26 September 2014. The couple welcomed their first child, daughter Aarya, in October 2019.

- Domestic career

Rahane had performed well when India U-19 toured New Zealand in early 2007, with two centuries. He was picked for the Mohammad Nissar Trophy in Pakistan.

- First-class career

Rahane made his first-class debut, at the age of 19, for Mumbai against Karachi Urban in the Mohammad Nissar Trophy in September 2007, at Karachi, when most of the first-choice Mumbai players were unavailable for various reasons. Opening the innings with Sahil Kukreja, he scored a century on debut 143 (207), with Kukreja scoring 110 for a total of 247. Rahane was subsequently picked for the Irani Trophy match against Rest of India.

- Rahane scored 172 against England Lions for West Zone in the 2007–08 Duleep Trophy.

Rahane, with 1089 runs in his second Ranji season (2008–09),was a crucial factor in Mumbai's 38th title win. His score of 265 not-out (batting at no. 3 for Mumbai) came against Hyderabad at Rajiv Gandhi International Stadium, Uppal in the 2009–10 season and also tournament. Rahane surpassed 1000 runs in three separate seasons, and scoring 152 in the 2011 Irani Trophy match against Rajasthan helped him get selected for India's Test squad.

In April 2019, Rahane joined Hampshire as their overseas player for two months of the season.

- List A career

Rahane made his List A debut for Mumbai against Delhi for the Vijay Hazare Trophy in March 2007. He contributed 61 runs to a 171-run partnership with former Indian opener Wasim Jaffer. Two centuries back to back in the Emerging Players Tournament in Australia brought him a place in the India ODI (One Day International) squad for the tour of England in 2011.

Rahane progressed through the Mumbai ranks and had also been a part of the Indian U-19 team and the India A. Rahane had also turned out for India Blue and India Green in the NKP Salve Challenger Trophy.

In September 2018, Rahane was named as the captain of Mumbai for the 2018–19 Vijay Hazare Trophy tournament. In October 2018, he was named as the captain of India C's squad for the 2018–19 Deodhar Trophy. He led the team to the final and played a crucial knock of 144* in the final to win the title.

- Test career

Rahane was selected in the Test squad to play against West Indies in November 2011. Rahane was taken in the squad for 16 months and in his presence, he saw seven players make their debuts. His performance in the limited-overs cricket (ODI and T20I) during that period was not up to the mark, as he averaged around 25 in both ODI and T20I cricket, and struggled for form in the series against Pakistan and England (in January 2013).

Rahane made his Test debut on 22 March 2013 against Australia in the Border-Gavaskar Trophy at Feroz Shah Kotla Stadium, Delhi. According to the media, Rahane got this chance through "sheer luck". Shikhar Dhawan, who made a dazzling start to his career in the third Test at Mohali, scoring 187 on debut, was the obvious choice for the Delhi Test until he suffered an injury to the knuckles of his left hand. Gautam Gambhir, who was picked as a replacement for Dhawan, was sidelined owing to jaundice. Rahane was handed his India Test cap which brought an end to a lean patch for Mumbai, who had not produced a Test player for India since May 2007. Two single-digit scores in the game prompted many to question Rahane's ability to handle pressure and replicate his domestic success at international level.

Despite his failure in the debut match, Rahane was included in the playing eleven for the first match of India's tour of South Africa (2013–14). Batting in the lower-middle order, he made 209 runs at an average of 69.66 in the series (including a 96 off 157 balls at Kingsmead, Durban) against the bowling attack comprising Dale Steyn, Morne Morkel and Vernon Philander. "For a man who had spent many a tour and series warming up the bench, carrying drinks, wondering when his opportunity will come, he has taken his chance with both hands, even though it arrived in the most difficult of conditions to bat in", cricket pundit Sidharth Monga wrote. Rahane finished as India's third-highest run-getter in the series, but he was in the most precarious position of all before the series began.

Rahane made his first Test ton at Basin Reserve, Wellington, New Zealand on 15 February 2014 against New Zealand. India were in a difficult position when Rahane came to the crease at 156 for five and by the time he departed with 118 India were in a match-winning position ruined by Brendon McCullum's famous triple-century. "He had a mountain of first-class runs backing him, of course, but did he have what goes around by the queer name of X-factor? Did he have that extra edge in his game and personality that separates top-class international players from the rest? Was he merely humble, or was he unable to assert himself, unable to absorb real pressure? After his first two Test tours to South Africa and New Zealand, we can safely conclude it must be the former. Underneath that seemingly soft exterior lurks a solid Test batsman, and he was on display at the Basin Reserve", ESPN Cricinfo wrote in their analysis.

Rahane played in the Investec Test Series (India tour of England, 2014) in England. His previous overseas performances (in away Tests, Rahane averaged 61.83 having scored 371 in four Tests including a century and two fifties) earned him a place in the playing eleven over Rohit Sharma. He justified his selection by making his second century at the second Test match at Lord's Cricket Ground. Put in to bat on a green-top wicket by Alastair Cook, India collapsed to 140 for six by tea, only to be rescued by Rahane's century. He was supported by Bhuvneshwar Kumar, who scored a valuable 36, besides putting on 90 runs for the eighth wicket.In the process, Rahane became the fourth Indian batsman to post a Test century on his first appearance at Lord's, joining Sourav Ganguly, Dilip Vengsarkar and Ajit Agarkar.

Rahane played in the 2014–15 Border-Gavaskar Trophy in Australia. In the third Test match at Melbourne, Rahane made his third Test hundred. He made 399 runs in four, including a century and three half-centuries against the opposition attack of Mitchell Johnson and Ryan Harris, the core of a bowling unit that famously won 2013–14 Ashes series 5–0.

In the first Test of 2015 tour of Sri Lanka, Rahane broke the world record for most catches in a Test match with eight. In the second Test at PSS, Colombo, he scored his fourth Test hundred, scoring 126 in India's second innings, and India went on to win the match. In the process, he reached his career-best ranking of 20th, at the ICC Player Rankings.

Rahane played in the 2015 Freedom Series. In the 4th test match at New Delhi, Rahane made centuries in both the innings on a pitch where most batsmen found it difficult to score, and with this feat, he became only the fifth Indian to join the elite club of twin centurions in a single test.

- On 16 August 2016, Rahane achieved his career best test batsmen's ranking of No. 8.

On 25 March 2017, Rahane became India's 33rd Test Captain when he led the team in the 4th test against Australia in Dharamsala due to an injury to Virat Kohli. He scored 46 runs in his first innings and quick 37 Runs in 2nd innings as India's Test captain. He scored a century in Sri Lanka in August 2017. In the return series at home, he failed miserably scoring only 17 in 5 innings. Despite an overseas average of 55, he was not included in the playing 11 for the 1st and 2nd Test against South Africa in 2018. After the failures of Rohit Sharma in both tests, the Indian vice-captain was brought back into the playing eleven for the 3rd test where his innings of 48 in the 2nd innings on a dangerous batting pitch proved very crucial in setting up an Indian victory.

He led the Indian Team in the test match against Afghanistan national cricket team in the absence of Virat Kohli in 2018. In the India's tour of England, Rahane scored two half centuries, a match winning 81 in the third test and 51 in the fourth test. In the following India's tour of Australia, Rahane scored two half centuries; a match-winning 70 in the Adelaide test and a 51 in the Perth test. Overall, he finished the series with 217 runs.

In 2019 two Match series in West Indies, he scored a century in the First Test to guide India to victory. In the home series against South Africa, he scored a brisk fifty in second Test in Pune sharing a crucial century partnership with skipper Virat Kohli. In the third Test, he scored a match winning 115 with a 267 run partnership with Rohit Sharma who scored his first double century in Tests rescuing the team from 39 for 3.

On 15 November 2019, in the first innings of the first test match against Bangladesh, Rahane hit 86 off 172 deliveries, crossing the boundary 9 times. This became his 21st test fifty in international cricket.

He was selected in the Test eleven for a 2 match series against New Zealand in February 2020, but like the rest of the team, his batting performance was not up to the mark.

In December 2020 he was made captain of the Indian teamfor the final three matches of India's tour of Australia in place of Virat Kohli, who was taking paternity leave. In the second test, Rahane scored 112 in the first innings and 27* in the second innings and guided India to a 8 wicket victory and was awarded man of the match.After drawing the third test at Sydney, India went on to win the fourth test in Brisbane and handed Australia their first Test defeat at The Gabba in 32 years with Rahane contributing to the winning cause with a quick fire 24 runs off 22 balls in the second innings and India winning the series 2–1. He finished the series as the third highest run getter with 268 runs at an average of 38.28. He received high praise from the critics and pundits for his captaincy and leading India to one of their greatest Test series win despite losing out on many of the first team players due to injury and bouncing back strongly after the first Test defeat. Rahane has captained India in 5 Tests, remaining unbeaten with 4 wins and a draw.

Rahane was appointed as the captain of the Indian team for the first Test against New Zealand in November 2021, as Kohli had been rested.

• One-Day International career

Two back to back centuries in the Emerging Players Tournament in Australia (201) helped Rahane secure a place in the India limited-overs squad for the tour of England. He made his debut against England at Chester-le-Street as a replacement for opener Virender Sehwag. Although Rahane made 40 runs at strike-rate of 90.90, India's hopes of their first victory of the 2011 summer against England were thwarted by a washout at Chester-le-Street.

He did well in his maiden international series (2011 NatWest Series), against England in England, and in the return series. He made a 47 ball 54 on his second match of the latter tour. Rahane failed to impress in his next few limited over matches against West Indies, Sri Lanka, Pakistan and England.

Rahane made his second ODI fifty in 2013-14 Asia Cup, only to be followed by another slump. In a short ODI career in the middle order, Rahane has seemed unsure and struggled at times to find the balance between defence and attack. He showed signs of comfort at the top of the order with rapid centuries against England (September 2014) and Sri Lanka (November 2014), but Rohit Sharma's second ODI double-century followed by a big hundred against Australia at the MCG pushed Rahane back to the middle order. T20sIn the ICC Cricket World Cup followed.

Rahane only managed to score 208 runs from 8 matches, with an average of 34.66. He was dropped by Mahendra Singh Dhoni in the second ODI against Bangladesh but after the series, he was appointed as captain of India for its tour of Zimbabwe for ODIs and T20Is in 2015 when a second string squad was selected. India won that ODI series 3–0, although Rahane was not able to leave any big impacts with the bat, he made a total of 112 in three matches with only one half-century in it.

• T20I career

Rahane made his international debut for India in a Twenty20 International against England at Old Trafford Cricket Ground, Manchester in August 2011. He scored a half-century on this match (61 of 49) against an England attack comprising Stuart Broad, Graeme Swann and Tim

Bresnan. The match was the only T20I played by former Indian captain Rahul Dravid.

Rahane was part of Indian team make it to the final of 2014 World T20. After sitting on the bench for the first three matches he got a chance to play against Australia where he scored 19 runs. He gave India a good start in the semi-final scoring 32 runs as India went on to win the Match. He also captained India in the two Twenty20 International against Zimbabwe, winning the first and losing the second match. He scored 33 and 4 runs in those matches.

- IPL career

Rahane with his Rajasthan Royals teammates in 2012

Rahane was picked by Rajasthan Royals on 2012 Indian premier league. Previously he was in the Mumbai Indians squads but got limited opportunities. And then, he caught the eye of Rajasthan Royals' Shane Watson, who had watched him score an 80-ball hundred in a session in the second innings of a three-day game against Australia A in 2010. Having bought him from the Mumbai Indians, Rahul Dravid and Watson got Rahane to open the innings. "Opening the batting with Rahul bhai gave me a chance to express myself and showcase all that I had learned over the years," Rahane explained.

- Ajinkya Rahane in IPL (2008–15)

Rahane has had a successful stint with Rajasthan Royals so far, playing under Rahul Dravid's mentorship.Rahane rose to prominence in the Premier League world in 2012 season for Rajasthan Royals. He hit a match-winning 98 in his first game of IPL 2012 against Kings XI Punjab and followed that up with an unbeaten 103 against Royal Challengers Bangalore.His 84 off 63 balls against Delhi Daredevils was in vain though, as they lost by one run. In Premier League 2012, Rahane became the first batsman to hit a century and emerged the leading run-scorer for Rajasthan Royals. He was retained by the Royals for the 2014 Premier League season.

Over the years, Rahul Dravid has been given a lot of credit for way Rahane has matured as a player. With Dravid guiding him, Rahane has transformed from a shy, long-format specialist into a player capable of batting at any position, in any format. Former India captain Sunil Gavaskar told NDTV, "What has been impressive about Rahane's career is the way he has made those little changes that have helped him to get better in every format of the game. This batsman is a thinking batsman, who keeps thinking about how to get better and that is why he is such a vital cog in the Rajasthan Royals team and a vital cog in the Indian cricket team."

Rahane had played for Rising Pune Supergiant in 2016 and 2017 season. Rahane was the leading run-scorer for RPS in 2016 season. Rahane had led RPS in a match against Delhi Daredevils in 2017 season when RPS captain Steve Smith missed out due to food poisoning.

In 2018, Rahane was brought back for Rs 4 crore by Rajasthan Royals by using a Right-to-Match card. Steve Smith was appointed as Captain of Rajasthan Royals on 24 February 2018. Following the ball tampering scandal against South Africa, Steve Smith who was the captain of Australia stepped down as Royals Captain. Rahane was set to lead Rajasthan Royals for the 2018 Season.

In 2012, Rahane came in limelight when he scored a magnificent century in IPL. The following years helped him join the international matches. IPL became worse for him in 2018, as compared to 2017. His strike rate came into talk and soon he became another Rahane. He is no more included in limited formats for international matches. IPL 2019 has been important for Rahane as he played some useful innings for team also smashed a century against Delhi capitals in SMS stadium in the 2019 season and became the highest run scorer for Rajasthan Royals (105*), this was his second century in IPL . In November 2019, Rahane was transferred from Rajasthan Royals to Delhi Capitals ahead of the 2020 Indian Premier League. The franchise has retained him for the IPL-2021 season.

CHAPTER TWO

Let's Know About Cricket

- Cricket

Cricket is a bat-and-ball game played between two teams of eleven players on a field at the centre of which is a 22-yard (20-metre) pitch with a wicket at each end, each comprising two bails balanced on three stumps. The game proceeds when a player on the fielding team, called the bowler, "bowls" (propels) the ball from one end of the pitch towards the wicket at the other end. The batting side's players score runs by striking the bowled ball with a bat and running between the wickets, while the bowling side tries to prevent this by keeping the ball within the field and getting it to either wicket, and dismiss each batter (so they are "out"). Means of dismissal include being bowled, when the ball hits the stumps and dislodges the bails, and by the fielding side either catching a hit ball before it touches the ground, or hitting a wicket with the ball before a batter can cross the crease line in front of the wicket to complete a run. When ten batters have been dismissed, the innings ends and the teams swap roles. The game is adjudicated by two umpires, aided by a third umpire and match referee in international matches.

Forms of cricket range from Twenty20, with each team batting for a single innings of 20 overs and the game generally lasting three hours, to Test matches played over five days. Traditionally cricketers play in all-white kit, but in limited overs cricket they wear club or team colours. In addition to the basic kit, some players wear protective gear to prevent injury caused by the ball, which is a hard, solid spheroid made of compressed leather with a slightly raised sewn seam enclosing a cork core layered with tightly wound string.

The earliest reference to cricket is in South East England in the mid-16th century. It spread globally with the expansion of the British Empire, with the first international matches in the second half of the 19th century. The game's governing body is the International Cricket Council (ICC), which has over 100 members, twelve of which are full members who play Test matches. The game's rules, the Laws of Cricket, are maintained by Marylebone Cricket Club (MCC) in London. The sport is followed primarily in South Asia, Australasia, the United Kingdom, southern Africa and the West Indies.Women's cricket, which is organised and played separately, has also achieved international standard. The most successful side playing international cricket is Australia, which has won seven One Day International trophies, including five World Cups, more than any other country and has been the top-rated Test side more than any other country.

- History of cricket to 1725

A medieval "club ball" game involving an underhand bowl towards a batter. Ball catchers are shown positioning themselves to catch a ball. Detail from the Canticles of Holy Mary, 13th century.

Cricket is one of many games in the "club ball" sphere that basically involve hitting a ball with a hand-held implement; others include baseball (which shares many similarities with cricket, both belonging in the more specific bat-and-ball games category), golf, hockey, tennis, squash, badminton and table tennis. In cricket's case, a key difference is the existence of a solid target structure, the wicket (originally, it is thought, a "wicket gate" through which sheep were herded), that the batter must defend. The cricket historian Harry Altham identified three "groups" of "club ball" games: the "hockey group", in which the ball is driven to and fro between two targets (the goals); the "golf group", in which the ball is driven towards an undefended target (the hole); and the "cricket group", in which "the ball is aimed at a mark (the wicket) and driven away from it".

It is generally believed that cricket originated as a children's game in the south-eastern counties of England, sometime during the medieval period.Although there are claims for prior dates, the earliest definite reference to cricket being played comes from evidence given at a court case in Guildford in January 1597 (Old Style), equating to January 1598 in the modern calendar. The case concerned ownership of a certain plot of land and the court heard the testimony of a 59-year-old coroner, John Derrick, who gave witness that.

Being a scholler in the ffree schoole of Guldeford hee and diverse of his fellows did runne and play there at creckett and other plaies.

Given Derrick's age, it was about half a century earlier when he was at school and so it is certain that cricket was being played c. 1550 by boys in Surrey. The view that it was originally a children's game is reinforced by Randle Cotgrave's 1611 English-French dictionary in which he defined the noun "crosse" as "the crooked staff wherewith boys play at cricket" and the verb form "crosser" as "to play at cricket".

One possible source for the sport's name is the Old English word "cryce" (or "cricc") meaning a crutch or staff. In Samuel Johnson's Dictionary, he derived cricket from "cryce, Saxon, a stick". In Old French, the word "criquet" seems to have meant a kind of club or stick. Given the strong medieval trade connections between south-east England and the County of Flanders when the latter belonged to the Duchy of Burgundy, the name may have been derived from the Middle Dutch (in use in Flanders at the time) "krick"(-e), meaning a stick (crook). Another possible source is the Middle Dutch word "krickstoel", meaning a long low stool used for kneeling in church and which resembled the long low wicket with two stumps used in early cricket. According to Heiner Gillmeister, a European language expert of Bonn University, "cricket" derives from the Middle Dutch phrase for hockey, met de (krik ket)sen (i.e., "with the stick chase"). Gillmeister has suggested that not only the name but also the sport itself may be of Flemish origin.

- Growth of amateur and professional cricket in England

Evolution of the cricket bat. The original "hockey stick" (left) evolved into the straight bat from c. 1760 when pitched delivery bowling began.

Although the main object of the game has always been to score the most runs, the early form of cricket differed from the modern game in certain key technical aspects; the North American variant of cricket known as wicket retained many of these aspects. The ball was bowled underarm by the bowler and along the ground towards a batter armed with a bat that in shape resembled a hockey stick; the batter defended a low, two-stump wicket; and runs were called notches because the scorers recorded them by notching tally sticks.

In 1611, the year Cotgrave's dictionary was published, ecclesiastical court records at Sidlesham in Sussex state that two parishioners, Bartholomew Wyatt and Richard Latter, failed to attend church on Easter Sunday because they were playing cricket. They were fined 12d each and ordered to do penance.This is the earliest mention of adult participation in cricket and it was around the same time that the earliest known organised inter-parish or village match was played – at Chevening, Kent. In 1624, a player called Jasper Vinall died after he was accidentally struck on the head during a match between two parish teams in Sussex.

Cricket remained a low-key local pursuit for much of the 17th century. It is known, through numerous references found in the records of ecclesiastical court cases, to have been proscribed at times by the Puritans before and during the Commonwealth. The problem was nearly always the issue of Sunday play as the Puritans considered cricket to be "profane" if played on the Sabbath, especially if large crowds or gambling were involved.

According to the social historian Derek Birley, there was a "great upsurge of sport after the Restoration" in 1660. Gambling on sport became a problem significant enough for Parliament to pass the 1664 Gambling Act, limiting stakes to £100 which was, in any case, a colossal sum exceeding the annual income of 99% of the population. Along with prizefighting, horse racing and blood sports, cricket was perceived to be a gambling sport.Rich patrons made matches for high stakes, forming teams in which they engaged the first professional players.By the end of the century, cricket had developed into a major sport that was spreading throughout England and was already being taken abroad by English mariners and colonisers – the earliest reference to cricket overseas is dated 1676. A 1697 newspaper report survives of "a great cricket match" played in Sussex "for fifty guineas apiece" – this is the earliest known contest that is generally considered a First Class match.

- The patrons, and other players from the social class known as the "gentry", began to classify themselves as "amateurs"[fn 1] to establish a clear distinction from the professionals, who were invariably members of the working class, even to the point of having separate changing and dining facilities. The gentry, including such high-ranking nobles as the Dukes of Richmond, exerted their honour code of noblesse oblige to claim rights of leadership in any sporting contests they took part in, especially as it was necessary for them to play alongside their "social inferiors" if they were to win their bets. In time, a perception took hold that the typical amateur who played in first-class cricket, until 1962 when amateurism was abolished, was someone with a public school education who had then gone to one of Cambridge or Oxford University – society insisted that such people were "officers and gentlemen" whose destiny was to provide leadership. In a purely financial sense, the cricketing amateur would theoretically claim expenses for playing while his professional counterpart played under contract and was paid a wage or match fee; in practice, many amateurs claimed more than actual expenditure and the derisive term "shamateur" was coined to describe the practice.

- The Young Cricketer, 1768

The game underwent major development in the 18th century to become England's national sport.Its success was underwritten by the twin necessities of patronage and betting. Cricket was prominent in London as early as 1707 and, in the middle years of the century, large crowds flocked to matches on the Artillery Ground in Finsbury. The single wicket form of the sport attracted huge crowds and wagers to match, its popularity peaking in the 1748 season. Bowling underwent an evolution around 1760 when bowlers began to pitch the ball instead of rolling or skimming it towards the batter. This caused a revolution in bat design because, to deal with the bouncing ball, it was necessary to introduce the modern straight bat in place of the old "hockey stick" shape.

The Hambledon Club was founded in the 1760s and, for the next twenty years until the formation of Marylebone Cricket Club (MCC) and the opening of Lord's Old Ground in 1787, Hambledon was both the game's greatest club and its focal point. MCC quickly became the sport's premier club and the custodian of the Laws of Cricket. New Laws introduced in the latter part of the 18th century included the three stump wicket and leg before wicket (lbw).

The 19th century saw underarm bowling superseded by first roundarm and then overarm bowling. Both developments were controversial.Organisation of the game at county level led to the creation of the county clubs, starting with Sussex in 1839. In December 1889, the eight leading county clubs formed the official County Championship, which began in 1890.

The most famous player of the 19th century was W. G. Grace, who started his long and influential career in 1865. It was especially during the career of Grace that the distinction between amateurs and professionals became blurred by the existence of players like him who were nominally amateur but, in terms of their financial gain, de facto professional. Grace himself was said to have been paid more money for playing cricket than any professional.

The last two decades before the First World War have been called the "Golden Age of cricket". It is a nostalgic name prompted by the collective sense of loss resulting from the war, but the period did produce some great players and memorable matches, especially as organised competition at county and Test level developed.

- Cricket becomes an international sport

In 1844, the first-ever international match took place between the United States and Canada. In 1859, a team of English players went to North America on the first overseas tour. Meanwhile, the British Empire had been instrumental in spreading the game overseas and by the middle of the 19th century it had become well established in Australia, the Caribbean, India, Pakistan, New Zealand, North America and South Africa.

In 1862, an English team made the first tour of Australia. The first Australian team to travel overseas consisted of Aboriginal stockmen who toured England in 1868. The first One Day International match was played on 5 January 1971 between Australia and England at the Melbourne Cricket Ground.

In 1876–77, an England team took part in what was retrospectively recognised as the first-ever Test match at the Melbourne Cricket Ground against Australia. The rivalry between England and Australia gave birth to The Ashes in 1882, and this has remained Test cricket's most famous contest. Test cricket began to expand in 1888–89 when South Africa played England.

- World cricket in the 20th century

The inter-war years were dominated by Australia's Don Bradman, statistically the greatest Test batter of all time. Test cricket continued to expand during the 20th century with the addition of the West Indies (1928), New Zealand (1930) and India (1932) before the Second World War and then Pakistan (1952), Sri Lanka (1982), Zimbabwe (1992), Bangladesh (2000), Ireland and Afghanistan (both 2018) in the post-war period. South Africa was banned from international cricket from 1970 to 1992 as part of the apartheid boycott.

- The rise of limited overs cricket

Cricket entered a new era in 1963 when English counties introduced the limited overs variant. As it was sure to produce a result, limited overs cricket was lucrative and the number of matches increased. The first Limited

Overs International was played in 1971 and the governing International Cricket Council (ICC), seeing its potential, staged the first limited overs Cricket World Cup in 1975. In the 21st century, a new limited overs form, Twenty20, made an immediate impact. On 22 June 2017, Afghanistan and Ireland became the 11th and 12th ICC full members, enabling them to play Test cricket.

- A typical cricket field.

In cricket, the rules of the game are specified in a code called The Laws of Cricket (hereinafter called "the Laws") which has a global remit. There are 42 Laws (always written with a capital "L"). The earliest known version of the code was drafted in 1744 and, since 1788, it has been owned and maintained by its custodian, the Marylebone Cricket Club (MCC) in London.

- Playing area

Cricket is a bat-and-ball game played on a cricket field (see image, right) between two teams of eleven players each. The field is usually circular or oval in shape and the edge of the playing area is marked by a boundary, which may be a fence, part of the stands, a rope, a painted line or a combination of these; the boundary must if possible be marked along its entire length.

In the approximate centre of the field is a rectangular pitch (see image, below) on which a wooden target called a wicket is sited at each end; the wickets are placed 22 yards (20 m) apart. The pitch is a flat surface 10 feet (3.0 m) wide, with very short grass that tends to be worn away as the game progresses (cricket can also be played on artificial surfaces, notably matting). Each wicket is made of three wooden stumps topped by two bails.

- Cricket pitch and creases

As illustrated above, the pitch is marked at each end with four white painted lines: a bowling crease, a popping crease and two return creases. The three stumps are aligned centrally on the bowling crease, which is eight feet eight inches long. The popping crease is drawn four feet in front of the bowling crease and parallel to it; although it is drawn as a twelve-foot line (six feet either side of the wicket), it is, in fact, unlimited in length. The return creases are drawn at right angles to the popping crease so that they intersect the ends of the bowling crease; each return crease is drawn as an eight-foot line, so that it extends four feet behind the bowling crease, but is also, in fact, unlimited in length.

Before a match begins, the team captains (who are also players) toss a coin to decide which team will bat first and so take the first innings. Innings is the term used for each phase of play in the match.In each innings, one team bats, attempting to score runs, while the other team bowls and fields the ball, attempting to restrict the scoring and dismiss the batters. When the first innings ends, the teams change roles; there can be two to four innings depending upon the type of match. A match with four scheduled innings is played over three to five days; a match with two scheduled innings is usually completed in a single day. During an innings, all eleven members of the fielding team take the field, but usually only two members of the batting team are on the field at any given time. The exception to this is if a batter has any type of illness or injury restricting his or her ability to run, in this case the batter is allowed a runner who can run between the wickets when the batter hits a scoring run or runs,though this does not apply in international cricket. The order of batters is usually announced just before the match, but it can be varied.

The main objective of each team is to score more runs than their opponents but, in some forms of cricket, it is also necessary to dismiss all of the opposition batters in their final innings in order to win the match, which would otherwise be drawn. If the team batting last is all out having scored fewer runs than their opponents, they are said to have "lost by n runs" (where n is the difference between the aggregate number of runs scored by the teams). If the team that bats last scores enough runs to win, it is said to have "won by n wickets", where n is the number of wickets left to fall. For example, a team that passes its opponents' total having lost six wickets (i.e., six of their batters have been dismissed) have won the match "by four wickets".

In a two-innings-a-side match, one team's combined first and second innings total may be less than the other side's first innings total. The team with the greater score is then said to have "won by an innings and n runs", and does not need to bat again: n is the difference between the two teams' aggregate scores. If the team batting last is all out, and both sides have scored the same number of runs, then the match is a tie; this result is quite rare in matches of two innings a side with only 62 happening in first-class matches from the earliest known instance in 1741 until January 2017. In the traditional form of the game, if the time allotted for the match expires before either side can win, then the game is declared a draw.

If the match has only a single innings per side, then a maximum number of overs applies to each innings. Such a match is called a "limited overs" or "one-day" match, and the side scoring more runs wins regardless of the number of wickets lost, so that a draw cannot occur. In some cases, ties are broken by having each team bat for a one-over innings known as a Super Over; subsequent Super Overs may be played if the first Super Over ends in a tie. If this kind of match is temporarily interrupted by bad weather, then a complex mathematical formula, known as the Duckworth–Lewis–Stern method after its developers, is often used to recalculate a new target score. A one-day match can also be declared a "no-result" if fewer than a previously agreed number of overs have been bowled by either team, in circumstances that make normal resumption of play impossible; for example, wet weather.

In all forms of cricket, the umpires can abandon the match if bad light or rain makes it impossible to continue. There have been instances of entire matches, even Test matches scheduled to be played over five days, being lost to bad weather without a ball being bowled: for example, the third Test of the 1970/71 series in Australia.

• Innings

The innings (ending with 's' in both singular and plural form) is the term used for each phase of play during a match. Depending on the type of match being played, each team has either one or two innings. Sometimes all eleven members of the batting side take a turn to bat but, for various reasons, an innings can end before they have all done so. The innings terminates if the batting team is "all out", a term defined by the Laws: "at the fall of a wicket or the retirement of a batter, further balls remain to be bowled but no further batter is available to come in". In this situation, one of the batters has not been dismissed and is termed not out; this is because he has no partners left and there must always be two active batters while the innings is in progress.

- An innings may end early while there are still two not out batters

the batting team's captain may declare the innings closed even though some of his players have not had a turn to bat: this is a tactical decision by the captain, usually because he believes his team have scored sufficient runs and need time to dismiss the opposition in their innings

the set number of overs (i.e., in a limited overs match) have been bowled

the match has ended prematurely due to bad weather or running out of time

in the final innings of the match, the batting side has reached its target and won the game.

- Overs

The Laws state that, throughout an innings, "the ball shall be bowled from each end alternately in overs of 6 balls". The name "over" came about because the umpire calls "Over!" when six balls have been bowled. At this point, another bowler is deployed at the other end, and the fielding side changes ends while the batters do not. A bowler cannot bowl two successive overs, although a bowler can (and usually does) bowl alternate overs, from the same end, for several overs which are termed a "spell". The batters do not change ends at the end of the over, and so the one who was non-striker is now the striker and vice versa. The umpires also change positions so that the one who was at "square leg" now stands behind the wicket at the non-striker's end and vice versa.

- Clothing and equipment

English cricketer W. G. Grace "taking guard" in 1883. His pads and bat are very similar to those used today. The gloves have evolved somewhat. Many modern players use more defensive equipment than were available to Grace, most notably helmets and arm guards.

The wicket-keeper (a specialised fielder behind the batter) and the batters wear protective gear because of the hardness of the ball, which can be delivered at speeds of more than 145 kilometres per hour (90 mph) and presents a major health and safety concern. Protective clothing includes pads (designed to protect the knees and shins), batting gloves or wicket-keeper's gloves for the hands, a safety helmet for the head and a box for male players inside the trousers (to protect the crotch area). Some batters wear additional padding inside their shirts and trousers such as thigh pads, arm pads, rib protectors and shoulder pads. The only fielders allowed to wear protective gear are those in positions very close to the batter (i.e., if they are alongside or in front of him), but they cannot wear gloves or external leg guards.

Subject to certain variations, on-field clothing generally includes a collared shirt with short or long sleeves; long trousers; woolen pullover (if needed); cricket cap (for fielding) or a safety helmet; and spiked shoes or boots to increase traction. The kit is traditionally all white and this remains the case in Test and first-class cricket but, in limited overs cricket, team colours are worn instead.

- Bat and ball

Two types of cricket ball, both of the same size:

i) A used white ball. White balls are mainly used in limited overs cricket, especially in matches played at night, under floodlights (left).

ii) A used red ball. Red balls are used in Test cricket, first-class cricket and some other forms of cricket (right).

The essence of the sport is that a bowler delivers (i.e., bowls) the ball from his or her end of the pitch towards the batter who, armed with a bat, is "on strike" at the other end (see next sub-section: Basic gameplay).

The bat is made of wood, usually Salix alba (white willow), and has the shape of a blade topped by a cylindrical handle. The blade must not be more than 4.25 inches (10.8 cm) wide and the total length of the bat not more than 38 inches (97 cm). There is no standard for the weight, which is usually between 2 lb 7 oz and 3 lb (1.1 and 1.4 kg).

The ball is a hard leather-seamed spheroid, with a circumference of 9 inches (23 cm). The ball has a "seam": six rows of stitches attaching the leather shell of the ball to the string and cork interior. The seam on a new ball is prominent and helps the bowler propel it in a less predictable manner. During matches, the quality of the ball deteriorates to a point where it is no longer usable; during the course of this deterioration, its behaviour in flight will change and can influence the outcome of the match. Players will, therefore, attempt to modify the ball's behaviour by modifying its physical properties. Polishing the ball and wetting it with sweat or saliva is legal, even when the polishing is deliberately done on one side only to increase the ball's swing through the air, but the acts of rubbing other substances into the ball, scratching the surface or picking at the seam are illegal ball tampering.

- Player roles

Basic gameplay: bowler to batter
During normal play, thirteen players and two umpires are on the field. Two of the players are batters and the rest are all eleven members of the fielding team. The other nine players in the batting team are off the field in the pavilion. The image with overlay below shows what is happening when a ball is being bowled and which of the personnel are on or close to the pitch.

- Return crease

In the photo, the two batters (3 & 8; wearing yellow) have taken position at each end of the pitch (6). Three members of the fielding team (4, 10 & 11; wearing dark blue) are in shot. One of the two umpires (1; wearing white hat) is stationed behind the wicket (2) at the bowler's (4) end of the pitch. The bowler (4) is bowling the ball (5) from his end of the pitch to the batter at the other end who is called the "striker". The other batter (3) at the bowling end is called the "non-striker". The wicket-keeper (10), who is a specialist, is positioned behind the striker's wicket (9) and behind him stands one of the fielders in a position called "first slip" (11). While the bowler and the first slip are wearing conventional kit only, the two batters and the wicket-keeper are wearing protective gear including safety helmets, padded gloves and leg guards (pads).

While the umpire (1) in shot stands at the bowler's end of the pitch, his colleague stands in the outfield, usually in or near the fielding position called "square leg", so that he is in line with the popping crease (7) at the striker's end of the pitch. The bowling crease (not numbered) is the one on which the wicket is located between the return creases (12). The bowler (4) intends to hit the wicket (9) with the ball (5) or, at least, to prevent the striker (8) from scoring runs. The striker (8) intends, by using his bat, to defend his wicket and, if possible, to hit the ball away from the pitch in order to score runs.

Some players are skilled in both batting and bowling, or as either or these as well as wicket-keeping, so are termed all-rounders. Bowlers are classified according to their style, generally as fast bowlers, seam bowlers or spinners. Batters are classified according to whether they are right-handed or left-handed.

- Fielding

Of the eleven fielders, three are in shot in the image above. The other eight are elsewhere on the field, their positions determined on a tactical basis by the captain or the bowler. Fielders often change position between deliveries, again as directed by the captain or bowler.

If a fielder is injured or becomes ill during a match, a substitute is allowed to field instead of him, but the substitute cannot bowl or act as a captain, except in the case of concussion substitutes in international cricket. The substitute leaves the field when the injured player is fit to return. The Laws of Cricket were updated in 2017 to allow substitutes to act as wicket-keepers.

- Bowling and dismissal

Glenn McGrath of Australia holds the world record for most wickets in the Cricket World Cup.

Most bowlers are considered specialists in that they are selected for the team because of their skill as a bowler, although some are all-rounders and even specialist batters bowl occasionally. The specialists bowl several times during an innings but may not bowl two overs consecutively. If the captain wants a bowler to "change ends", another bowler must temporarily fill in so that the change is not immediate.

A bowler reaches his delivery stride by means of a "run-up" and an over is deemed to have begun when the bowler starts his run-up for the first delivery of that over, the ball then being "in play".

Fast bowlers, needing momentum, take a lengthy run up while bowlers with a slow delivery take no more than a couple of steps before bowling. The fastest bowlers can deliver the ball at a speed of over 145 kilometres per hour (90 mph) and they sometimes rely on sheer speed to try to defeat the batter, who is forced to react very quickly.

Other fast bowlers rely on a mixture of speed and guile by making the ball seam or swing (i.e. curve) in flight. This type of delivery can deceive a batter into miscuing his shot, for example, so that the ball just touches the edge of the bat and can then be "caught behind" by the wicket-keeper or a slip fielder. At the other end of the bowling scale is the spin bowler who bowls at a relatively slow pace and relies entirely on guile to deceive the batter. A spinner will often "buy his wicket" by "tossing one up" (in a slower, steeper parabolic path) to lure the batter into making a poor shot. The batter has to be very wary of such deliveries as they are often "flighted" or spun so that the ball will not behave quite as he expects and he could be "trapped" into getting himself out. In between the pacemen and the spinners are the medium paced seamers who rely on persistent accuracy to try to contain the rate of scoring and wear down the batter's concentration.

There are nine ways in which a batter can be dismissed: five relatively common and four extremely rare. The common forms of dismissal are bowled, caught, leg before wicket (lbw), run out and stumped. Rare methods are hit wicket,hit the ball twice, obstructing the field and timed out. The Laws state that the fielding team, usually the bowler in practice, must appeal for a dismissal before the umpire can give his decision. If the batter is out, the umpire raises a forefinger and says "Out!"; otherwise, he will shake his head and say "Not out".There is, effectively, a tenth method of dismissal, retired out, which is not an on-field dismissal as such but rather a retrospective one for which no fielder is credited.

- Batting, runs and extras

The directions in which a right-handed batter, facing down the page, intends to send the ball when playing various cricketing shots. The diagram for a left-handed batter is a mirror image of this one.

Batters take turns to bat via a batting order which is decided beforehand by the team captain and presented to the umpires, though the order remains flexible when the captain officially nominates the team. Substitute batters are generally not allowed, except in the case of concussion substitutes in international cricket.

In order to begin batting the batter first adopts a batting stance. Standardly, this involves adopting a slight crouch with the feet pointing across the front of the wicket, looking in the direction of the bowler, and holding the bat so it passes over the feet and so its tip can rest on the ground near to the toes of the back foot.

A skilled batter can use a wide array of "shots" or "strokes" in both defensive and attacking mode. The idea is to hit the ball to the best effect with the flat surface of the bat's blade. If the ball touches the side of the bat it is called an "edge". The batter does not have to play a shot and can allow the ball to go through to the wicketkeeper. Equally, he does not have to attempt a run when he hits the ball with his bat. Batters do not always seek to hit the ball as hard as possible, and a good player can score runs just by making a deft stroke with a turn of the wrists or by simply "blocking" the ball but directing it away from fielders so that he has time to take a run. A wide variety of shots are played, the batter's repertoire including strokes named according to the style of swing and the direction aimed: e.g., "cut", "drive", "hook", "pull".

The batter on strike (i.e. the "striker") must prevent the ball hitting the wicket, and try to score runs by hitting the ball with his bat so that he and his partner have time to run from one end of the pitch to the other before the fielding side can return the ball. To register a run, both runners must touch the ground behind the popping crease with either their bats or their bodies (the batters carry their bats as they run). Each completed run increments the score of both the team and the striker.

- Sachin Tendulkar is the only player to have scored one hundred international centuries

The decision to attempt a run is ideally made by the batter who has the better view of the ball's progress, and this is communicated by calling: usually "yes", "no" or "wait". More than one run can be scored from a single hit: hits worth one to three runs are common, but the size of the field is such that it is usually difficult to run four or more. To compensate for this, hits that reach the boundary of the field are automatically awarded four runs if the ball touches the ground en route to the boundary or six runs if the ball clears the boundary without touching the ground within the boundary. In these cases the batters do not need to run. Hits for five are unusual and generally rely on the help of "overthrows" by a fielder returning the ball. If an odd number of runs is scored by the striker, the two batters have changed ends, and the one who was non-striker is now the striker. Only the striker can score individual runs, but all runs are added to the team's total.

Additional runs can be gained by the batting team as extras (called "sundries" in Australia) due to errors made by the fielding side. This is achieved in four ways: no-ball, a penalty of one extra conceded by the bowler if he breaks the rules; wide, a penalty of one extra conceded by the bowler if he bowls so that the ball is out of the batter's reach bye, an extra awarded if the batter misses the ball and it goes past the wicket-keeper and gives the batters time to run in the conventional way leg bye, as for a bye except that the ball has hit the batter's body, though not his bat. If the bowler has conceded a no-ball or a wide, his team incurs an additional penalty because that ball (i.e., delivery) has to be bowled again and hence the batting side has the opportunity to score more runs from this extra ball.

• Specialist roles

Captain (cricket) and Wicket-keeper

The captain is often the most experienced player in the team, certainly the most tactically astute, and can possess any of the main skillsets as a batter, a bowler or a wicket-keeper. Within the Laws, the captain has certain responsibilities in terms of nominating his players to the umpires before the match and ensuring that his players conduct themselves "within the spirit and traditions of the game as well as within the Laws".

The wicket-keeper (sometimes called simply the "keeper") is a specialist fielder subject to various rules within the Laws about his equipment and demeanour. He is the only member of the fielding side who can effect a stumping and is the only one permitted to wear gloves and external leg guards. Depending on their primary skills, the other ten players in the team tend to be classified as specialist batters or specialist bowlers. Generally, a team will include five or six specialist batters and four or five specialist bowlers, plus the wicket-keeper.

- Umpires and scorers

Umpire (cricket), Scoring (cricket), and Cricket statistics

An umpire signals a decision to the scorers

The game on the field is regulated by the two umpires, one of whom stands behind the wicket at the bowler's end, the other in a position called "square leg" which is about 15–20 metres away from the batter on strike and in line with the popping crease on which he is taking guard. The umpires have several responsibilities including adjudication on whether a ball has been correctly bowled (i.e., not a no-ball or a wide); when a run is scored; whether a batter is out (the fielding side must first appeal to the

umpire, usually with the phrase "How's that?" or "Owzat?");
when intervals start and end; and the suitability of the
pitch, field and weather for playing the game. The umpires
are authorised to interrupt or even abandon a match due
to circumstances likely to endanger the players, such as a
damp pitch or deterioration of the light.

Off the field in televised matches, there is usually a third
umpire who can make decisions on certain incidents with
the aid of video evidence. The third umpire is mandatory
under the playing conditions for Test and Limited Overs
International matches played between two ICC full
member countries. These matches also have a match
referee whose job is to ensure that play is within the Laws
and the spirit of the game.

The match details, including runs and dismissals, are
recorded by two official scorers, one representing each
team. The scorers are directed by the hand signals of an
umpire . For example, the umpire raises a forefinger to
signal that the batter is out (has been dismissed); he raises
both arms above his head if the batter has hit the ball for
six runs. The scorers are required by the Laws to record all
runs scored, wickets taken and overs bowled; in practice,
they also note significant amounts of additional data
relating to the game.

A match's statistics are summarised on a scorecard.
Prior to the popularisation of scorecards, most scoring was
done by men sitting on vantage points cuttings notches
on tally sticks and runs were originally called
notches.According to Rowland Bowen, the earliest known
scorecard templates were introduced in 1776 by T. Pratt
of Sevenoaks and soon came into general use.It is believed
that scorecards were printed and sold at Lord's for the first
time in 1846.

thank you for buy & read this book
have a great day of your

www.ingramcontent.com/pod-product-compliance
Lightning Source LLC
Chambersburg PA
CBHW070206160726
47997CB00017B/1495